This book is dedicated to all of the Liam Llamas
out there with big and small worries.

www.mascotbooks.com

Llamaste

©2021 Keri Powers. All Rights Reserved. No part of this publication may be reproduced, stored in a retrieval system or transmitted in any form by any means electronic, mechanical, or photocopying, recording or otherwise without the permission of the author.

For more information, please contact:
Mascot Books
620 Herndon Parkway, Suite 320
Herndon, VA 20170
info@mascotbooks.com

Library of Congress Control Number: 2021903348

CPSIA Code: PRT0321A
ISBN-13: 978-1-64543-590-7

Printed in the United States

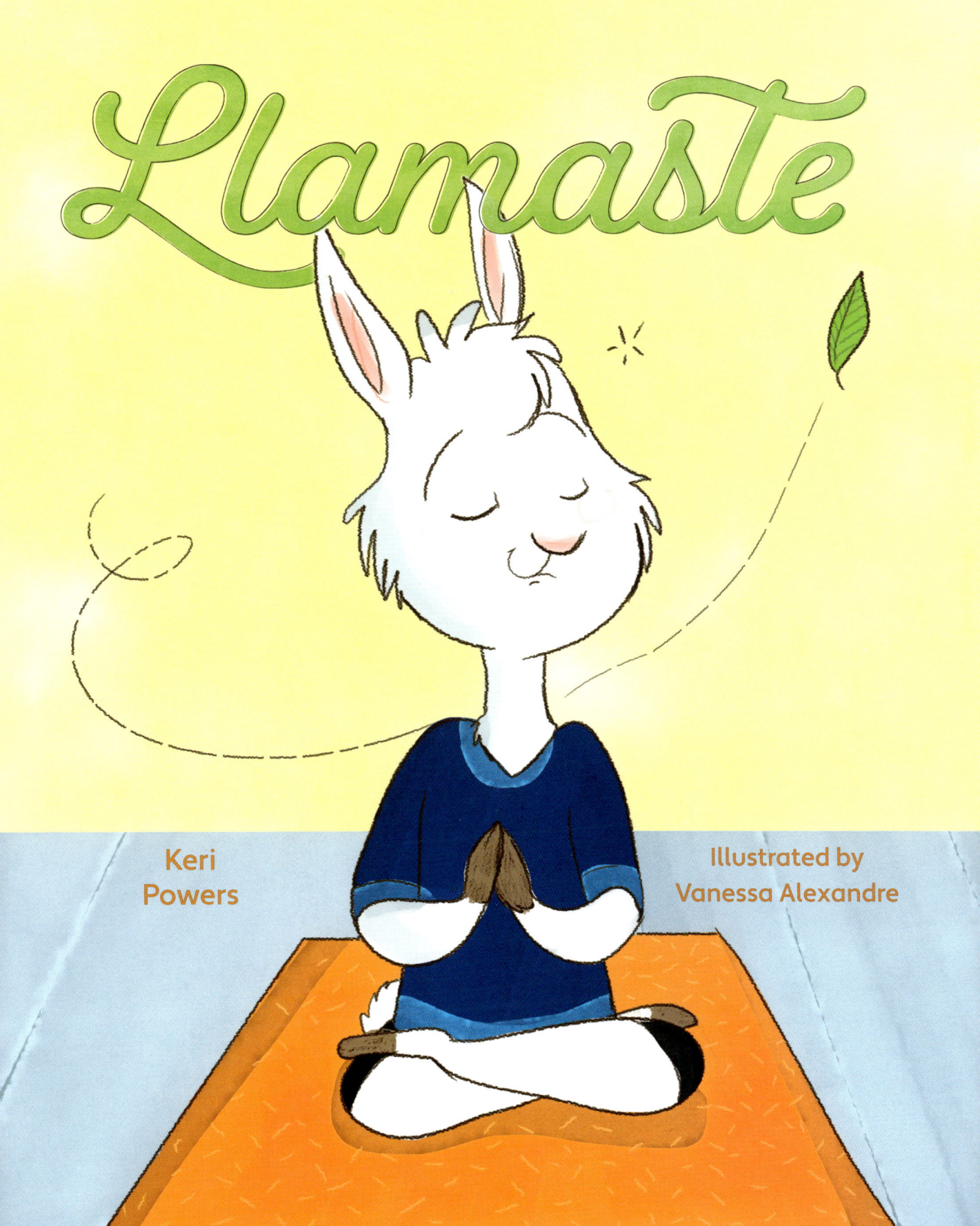

Liam was a Llama, and I really must say,
he spent his time worrying most of the day.
He worried about tomorrow. He worried about the past.
He worried about how long the worries would last.

He worried about spiders. He worried about the dark.
He worried about the beach and if there were sharks.

The worries sent Liam's head in a spin
and made it hard for calm thoughts to even get in.

His stomach felt all tied up in knots,
and his hands were always sweating a lot.
Liam's heart would pound, his throat felt tight,
and he knew this wasn't truly alright.

Then one day, Liam decided enough was enough.
He was finally ready to talk about stuff.
His mom listened and cared and made a suggestion:
"Let's practice yoga to feel grounded and do some reflection."

They sat and they breathed with their legs gently crossed.
They inhaled and exhaled and let go of worried thoughts.

EASY POSE

They folded their bodies and stretched their arms out, releasing the worries from the fingertip route.

I release you, my worries.

CHILD'S POSE

As they bent their bodies into a flexible hold,
they let other possibilities and ideas unfold.

DOWNWARD-FACING DOG POSE

They searched for new thoughts that could fill Liam's mind: true thoughts, real thoughts, and calm thoughts to unwind.

I am safe in this moment.

UPWARD-FACING DOG POSE

They stood tall and firm and welcomed thoughts that were real.
Maybe the beach wasn't really a big deal!

Tuning in to his body and honoring his strength reminded this llama of his courage at length.

Liam the Llama still worries from time to time. Like what if there's a giant alien covered in slime?

But he interrupts those worries with breathing and power.
His worries no longer last for hours and hours.
Now, Liam blends yoga into his day.
He lets worries go with a gentle, "Llamaste!"

ABOUT THE AUTHOR

Keri Powers began her career as a mental health counselor and quickly realized she loved working with children. Now, Keri is a K-6 school counselor and author who is passionate about helping kids understand and manage feelings of worry. Her first book, *Zen Hen*, helps kids understand and use mindful practices to calm their bodies and minds and connect to their present environment. Keri grew up in Georgia and attended Furman University and The George Washington University. She now lives on the beautiful island of Oahu and loves to spend time at the beach with her bulldogs Genevieve and James.